Coronado's
Golden
Quest

Published by Steck-Vaughn Company.

Text, illustrations, and cover art copyright © 1993 by Dialogue
Systems, Inc., 627 Broadway, New York, New York 10012.
All rights reserved.

Cover art by Mike Eagle

Printed in the United States of America
1 2 3 4 5 6 7 8 9 R 98 97 96 95 94 93 92

Library of Congress Cataloging-in-Publication Data

Weisberg, Barbara.
    Coronado's golden quest / author, Barbara Weisberg; illustrator,
Mike Eagle.
        p. cm.—(Stories of America)
    Includes bibliographical references.
    Summary: Describes Coronado's search for gold in the
American Southwest and his interaction with the Native
Americans there.
    ISBN 0-8114-7232-9 (hardcover).—ISBN 0-8114-8072-0 (soft-
cover)
    1. Coronado, Francisco Vásquez de, 1510–1554—Juvenile litera-
ture. 2. Southwest, New—Gold discoveries—Juvenile literature.
3. Southwest, New—Discovery and exploration—Spanish—
Juvenile literature. 4. Indians of North America—Southwest,
New—First contact with Europeans—Juvenile literature. 5.
Explorers—America—Biography—Juvenile literature. 6.
Explorers—Spain—Biography—Juvenile literature. [1. Coronado,
Francisco Vásquez de, 1510–1554. 2. Explorers. 3. Southwest,
New—Discovery and exploration. 4. America—Discovery and
exploration.] I. Eagle, Michael, ill. II. Title. III. Series.
E125.V3W45 1993
917.904'102—dc20   92–18078
[B]   CIP
                                                         AC

ISBN 0-8114-7232-9 (Hardcover)
ISBN 0-8114-8072-0 (Softcover)

Coronado's
Golden
Quest

by Barbara Weisberg
Alex Haley, General Editor

Illustrations by Mike Eagle

STECK-VAUGHN
C O M P A N Y
A Subsidiary of National Education Corporation

Introduction
by Alex Haley, General Editor

Over 450 years ago, New Spain was the center of the Spanish Empire in North America. It was an empire built on conquest. Its wealth was taken from the conquered Aztecs of Mexico and the Incas of Peru.

Then reports came into New Spain of great cities of gold to the north. General Francisco Coronado was sent to find these cities and to claim their wealth for the Spanish king. Coronado led an enormous army of exploration and conquest into what is now the Southwest of the United States.

Coronado's Golden Quest tells the story of the search for the cities of gold. Once this would have been a simple adventure story. But today we know that the stories of our past are almost never simple. We know that there is almost always more than one side to a story.

Barbara Weisberg's book describes the hardships Coronado and his army encounter. But it also describes the hardships *they* bring to the people whose lands they have invaded. It tells of the courage and determination of the Spanish soldiers. And it tells of the courage and determination of the Cicuyans and Quiverans as they resist the Spanish conquerors.

It remains an exciting adventure story. It's just not a simple one.

For Abby and Sarah

Contents

1

Sad Surprises

The horses pawed the red earth, restless to start the long journey ahead. Their riders stood quietly beside them. Even though the August sun blazed, some of the men wore coats of shiny metal armor. Others wore jackets of stiff leather. The little group had to be prepared for anything. Danger would shadow the long journey home. They had left their homes in the Spanish colony of New Spain six months before, in February 1540. Now, home lay more than a thousand miles south, across harsh wilderness and desert.

Juan Gallego, the leader of the assembled riders, shielded his eyes against the sun and looked toward the pueblo. The small, walled village

1

baked in the dry heat. The men were waiting for their general, Francisco Vázquez de Coronado, to bid them farewell. But where was Coronado? Gallego looked around. It wasn't like the General to be late. Just then, Gallego saw a glint of gold. Coronado was coming at last.

Gallego watched with affection as the General walked toward them. Coronado looked like a god in his golden armor. His blond hair gleamed almost as brightly as the metal, and his eyes shone. Coronado was a kind man and a brave general. He was fierce in battle and loyal to his followers. He tried to treat the people he conquered fairly. But Coronado worried Gallego these days. He seemed tired, very tired. In fact, he seemed older than his thirty years. Gallego, who was over fifty, sometimes felt Coronado was like his own son.

Coronado had chosen Gallego carefully for the long ride ahead. Despite his age, Gallego was very tough. He had the reputation of a tiger. He could be trusted with any duty, no matter how difficult or dangerous. Coronado greeted him warmly. Then the General put his hand on the neck of Gallego's horse and stroked the sleek velvet.

Coronado, an expert horseman, loved these

beautiful animals, which had been brought by the Spanish to New Spain. There were no horses in the north, except the ones that belonged to Coronado's soldiers. Coronado sometimes wondered how his soldiers could have managed without them. Horses made it possible to travel quickly and hunt efficiently. And the horses were a great help in battle. The people of these regions had never seen such animals before. They were stunned at the sight of armed, warlike men on the backs of thundering, four-legged beasts.

Ride as quickly as possible, Coronado ordered the men. They proudly nodded their agreement. They were messengers and knew how important this mission was. It was their duty to carry gifts and an official report from Coronado to Viceroy Antonio de Mendoza, head of the government of New Spain. Mendoza would then send the report across the ocean to the ruler of the Spanish Empire, Charles V, the King of Spain.

Coronado and Gallego exchanged glances. This was not going to be easy. Everyone knew Mendoza would be bitterly disappointed with the report. It had been Mendoza's idea to send Coronado and a vast army north in search of gold. Mendoza had heard that seven wealthy, golden cities, called Cibola, existed in the north. Mendoza hoped Coronado would find as much gold in Cibola as Hernando Cortés had found in Mexico and as Francisco Pizarro had found in Peru.

Viceroy Mendoza had spent his personal fortune to pay for the army. Its size and grandeur might have impressed even the kings and queens of Europe. A thousand people had volunteered, including more than two hundred Spanish soldiers. They had carried guns, swords, maces, and crossbows. Hundreds of Indian allies, many dressed in magnificent robes of parrot feathers, had joined the Spanish. A few women—wives of some of the soldiers—had decided to go along. A number of black and Indian servants and slaves also had accompanied the expedition. Behind the troops had trailed herds of mules, cows, sheep, goats, and hogs.

When the army had started out from New Spain six months before, in February 1540, it had been a glorious sight. Brightly colored banners had waved in the breeze, and the sound of trumpets had been heard far and wide. Since then, the army had met only hardships and sad surprises. The journey had led them up and down steep cliffs and across brutal deserts. Several men and

many animals had died from accidents or illness. And when at last the army had reached Cibola, they found no gold—no gold at all. Instead of seven huge, wealthy cities, they had discovered seven dusty little villages.

These events were described in Coronado's report to Mendoza. Coronado had struggled over it for days. It had been a hard letter to write, because the news was so bad. The people of Cibola had fiercely attacked the newcomers. "They knocked me down to the ground twice with countless great stones which they threw from above," Coronado wrote. "And if I had not been protected by the very good headpiece which I wore, I think that the outcome would have been very bad for me."

Coronado's army had finally defeated the inhabitants of Cibola, and the Cibolans had fled. Afterward, they had agreed to meet with Coronado. The Spanish and the Cibolans had exchanged gifts and made peace. "They declare it was foretold among them more than fifty years ago," Coronado told Mendoza, "that a people such as we are should come, and the direction they should come from, and that the whole country would be conquered."

Coronado had hoped to find streets paved with gold and jewels in Cibola. But there were no treasures in the dusty streets, no treasures anywhere. Yet, almost against his will, Coronado was impressed with the simple pueblos. The villages had sturdy walls and houses. "For although they are not decorated with turquoises nor made of lime nor good bricks, nevertheless they are very good houses, with three and four stories."

But there was no disguising the unpleasant facts. Coronado wanted to be honest with Mendoza, without destroying all hope. "As far as I can judge, it does not appear to me that there is any hope of getting gold or silver, but I trust in God that, if there is any, we shall get our share of it."

Although there was no gold in Cibola, who knew what the territory around might hold? No Europeans had ever explored these lands before. Coronado wrote that he planned to keep on searching for treasures. "I have determined to send throughout all the surrounding regions, in order to find out whether there is anything, and to suffer every extremity[1] before I give up this enterprise." The report concluded with typical

---

[1]danger or hardship

7

respect, "Francisco Vázquez de Coronado kisses the hand of your most illustrious Lordship."

Now, with the sun high in the sky, Coronado handed the sealed report to Gallego. The General had just finished it that morning, August 3, 1540. But the report wasn't the reason he had made the messengers wait. He had also been working on another letter, one that in some ways mattered just as much. He took Gallego aside and gave him the second letter.

Gallego already knew who it was for. He knew how much the General missed his wife Doña Beatriz. He told Coronado that he would be happy to deliver this letter to the General's wife. Gallego promised that only death would prevent him from fulfilling his mission.

Satisfied, Coronado turned back to the others. Once again he inspected the gifts he was sending to Mendoza. They included cloths painted with pictures of animals, earrings decorated with shiny turquoises, wicker baskets, a shield, a hammer, a bow, and some arrows. Coronado touched the delicate baskets and held the pretty earrings up to the light. These objects showed how the Cibolans lived, and Coronado thought they were interesting. But he knew the black-eyed, black-bearded Mendoza would be furious. Mendoza expected gold. Mountains of precious gold.

Everything was in order for the journey. Coronado saluted the messengers and wished them luck. He watched them ride off, disappearing in clouds of red dust. He wanted to be one of them, on the way home to New Spain and his beloved wife. His head lowered in sadness. I have left so much behind, he said to himself. Will I ever see my family again? Then he shook his head, as if waking from a dream. His duty lay here, he reminded himself. He must set an example for the others to follow. In his mind, he could see the image of the tawny lion wearing its shining crown. This image—the lion crowned—was the coat of arms of Coronado's distinguished family. It decorated their banners and shields. Whenever he thought about the lion, it inspired him.

Coronado walked back toward the little village. Called Hawikuh, it was the main pueblo of Cibola. His army was now camped within and around its walls. How thin and exhausted my soldiers are, Coronado thought, as he passed among them. How long can they go on without finding some reward? A soldier saluted him. The young

man stood straight and stern, but his face looked yellow and ill. Coronado knew that peril and disappointment still lay ahead. How many will survive? he wondered. And how many will die in these rugged, foreign lands? Will we find gold to satisfy our Viceroy and our King?

2

Keys to Splendid Treasures

Throughout the summer, with Hawikuh as his headquarters, Coronado sent men to explore in different directions. He told his soldiers to be friendly toward everyone they met. He wanted the peoples of the area to understand that the Spanish did not plan to harm them. Mendoza had given strict orders about this. Over time, Mendoza hoped all Indians would accept the King of Spain as their ruler and the Christian faith as their religion. But he did not want them to be treated cruelly, the way Pizarro and Cortés had treated them. Coronado strongly supported the Viceroy in this.

In a surprisingly short time, Coronado's messages succeeded. One day in late August he heard a great commotion. When he went to find out what was happening, he discovered several of his soldiers talking in sign language with a group of Indians. Everyone was shouting and waving their hands wildly.

As Coronado walked forward to greet the visitors, he felt a burst of sudden hope. He had never seen these Indians before. Perhaps they would be the ones who held the key to splendid treasures. Perhaps they knew where, in this vast land, there were golden cities. Let them enter, he ordered his men. With his strong hands, Coronado made a gesture of welcome.

The Indians' leader was a tall young man with an open and handsome face. Yet there was something quite surprising about his appearance. Unlike most of the Indians Coronado had met, the young chief had a long, drooping mustache. In his mind, Coronado immediately nicknamed him Whiskers. He also decided the man must come from a village of warriors, for the young chief carried a bow, arrows, a sharp spear, and a large shield with a brilliant red design on it. Everyone with him also carried weapons.

With the help of interpreters and hand gestures, Coronado and the visitors were able to talk. Where do you come from? Coronado asked.

The young man looked at Coronado as carefully as Coronado had looked at him. Such yellow hair! he thought. Such pale skin! But after a moment, the chief saw that Coronado had eyes that shone like a mountain lion's. Slowly, the young man began to speak, using sign language very clearly, so there was no trouble understanding.

We are from Cicuye, he told Coronado, which lies many days' journey away. He pointed east, toward the direction the sun rose. He explained that, as Coronado had guessed, Cicuye was a town of great warriors. The people of Cicuye had conquered many other villages, the young man continued, but had never been conquered themselves. His eyes shot a warning in Coronado's direction.

Coronado wondered if the chief was threatening war or just telling the army to stay away from his territory. Why are you here? Coronado demanded. What is the purpose of this visit?

We have traded for many years with the people of this village, the Cicuyan chief answered. A short time ago, they brought word to us that bold men had defeated them in battle. Now they say these bold strangers want to be friends. We have come to see for ourselves who these bold strangers are.

He paused. Coronado waited. Then the chief waved to the Cicuyans who stood behind him, and they began placing piles of shields and woolly animal skins in front of Coronado. These are gifts for you, said the chief. You have sent messages of friendship throughout the land. The people of Cicuye accept your offer.

Coronado felt relieved, pleased, and curious all at once. With smiles and gestures, he thanked the chief for his generosity. Then he leaned forward and held up one of the skins. But what kind of skins are these? he asked.

In response, Whiskers pointed to a tattoo on the arm of one of the Indians. Coronado examined the tattoo with amazement. It showed a large, shaggy beast a little like a cow—but this cow had a hump like a camel and a beard like a goat. We have heard about these beasts, said Coronado wonderingly, but no one in my army has ever seen one.

Whiskers nodded. None of the Cicuyans had ever seen horses before that morning, so it didn't

surprise him that Coronado had never seen the hump-back cows. These animals roam across the huge plains east of Cicuye, the chief explained. There are more of these beasts than stars in the sky! Then he invited Coronado to send some soldiers to visit Cicuye and see the great animals of the plains. Coronado immediately accepted. Afterwards, Coronado gave the young chief presents of glass beads and bells and invited him to stay at Cibola for several days.

The next morning, Coronado, as usual, went for a gallop on his favorite horse. The dawn air and swift ride always helped him think. As he trotted back from the rocky cliffs around Cibola, he struggled with a question.

Whiskers had said nothing about gold, but that didn't mean there wasn't any. Here was an exciting chance to explore under the protection of the helpful young chief. But who would be the best person to send?

He himself still had responsibilities in Cibola. López de Cárdenas, his army-master, or second-in-command, was a determined and experienced soldier. Cárdenas had taken part in many difficult expeditions in New Spain. But he was about to leave to explore the areas west of Cibola with a small group of twelve men. Melchior Diaz, Coronado's most trusted captain, was far to the south, searching for a route to the ocean. And Pedro de Tovar, almost as dependable, had just returned after exploring the areas northwest of Cibola. He was worn out and needed rest.

Coronado was very tempted to send Hernando de Alvarado, but he wasn't certain Alvarado had enough experience. Alvarado was very young, just a little over twenty-three. Still, he had handled his duties well as Captain of Artillery. And Coronado also felt in his debt. During the battle of Cibola, when Coronado lay wounded, Cárdenas and Alvarado had thrown themselves on his body. They had protected him from arrows and saved his life.

By the time Coronado rode back to camp, he had made up his mind. He dismounted and turned the horse over to its groom to be brushed. He patted its sweaty flanks and tweaked its pointed ear. Alvarado, he told the panting animal, is the man we will send to Cicuye.

3

Iron Collars and Gold Bracelets

On August 29, Hernando de Alvarado and twenty men set out for Cicuye with Whiskers. Coronado had given Alvarado eighty days to explore the lands east of Cibola. After that, Coronado ordered, it will be time to return.

Alvarado's heart pounded with excitement as he rode away from the walled pueblo of Hawikuh. This was his chance to make his name as a great captain in Coronado's army. He would be the first in the army to travel the plains and see the mysterious beasts that looked like cows. Perhaps he also would be the one to discover cities of gold. Alvarado's proud horse galloped far ahead of the others. Next to Coronado, Alvarado had the strongest and most handsome horses in the army.

The way eastward to Cicuye was long and difficult. In most places, there was little water. The hardy group of soldiers and Cicuyans traveled for days over dry, sunbaked desert. Sometimes they saw only lizards and mountain lions. But sometimes they came upon walled villages like those of Cibola. Wherever they went, Whiskers told the people to come out from their homes in peace. Because Whiskers' honesty and generosity were known far and wide, the people of the villages listened to him and welcomed the newcomers.

One place in particular impressed Alvarado. It was the district of Tiguex, located on a beautiful river. As soon as possible, Alvarado sat down to write a letter to Coronado. "This river of *Nuestra Señora*," Alvarado reported, "flows through a broad valley planted with fields of maize and dotted with cottonwood groves. There are twelve pueblos, whose houses are built of mud and are two stories high." He described how the people of the district had greeted them. "They marched around our tent, playing a flute, and with an old man for spokesman. In this manner they came inside the tent and presented me with food, cotton cloth, and skins which they had."

Alvarado liked Tiguex so well that he suggested Coronado spend the winter in one of the pretty villages there. Tiguex, Alvarado wrote, had more food and water than Cibola. Its resources could better support the army during the harsh winter months.

Alvarado and Whiskers arrived at Cicuye in late September, about a month after leaving Cibola. They had seen many interesting sights, but they were weary from the journey and badly in need of rest and supplies.

News of their coming had already reached Cicuye. As they approached the pueblo, Alvarado could see it was far larger than any of the villages they had visited. Suddenly men and women appeared along the top of the pueblo's high walls and scrambled down its ladders to the ground. They marched around the town playing flutes and drums and singing joyful songs of welcome. They were happy to have their chief back home.

The celebration made a strong impact on Whiskers. That evening he talked with Alvarado. I have been away too long, he said with regret.

It would not be wise for me to leave again immediately. The plains, Whiskers told Alvarado, lie another several days' journey away. He promised to give Alvarado two very good guides to take him there, men who knew the plains well. Then he summoned the two guides to meet Alvarado.

Alvarado nicknamed the first guide "The Turk." To Alvarado, the guide looked like a Turk, for he wore a turban wound around his head. The second guide was named Sopete. Sopete wore painted circles around his eyes, which gave him a bold, curious expression. Both men, said Whiskers, came from the other side of the plains, from a large district of many settlements. It was called Quivera. Both guides had been taken captive by Whiskers and were now servants in Cicuye.

While Whiskers related their stories, the Turk and Sopete glared at one another. Even at this first meeting, Alvarado could feel cold hatred bristling between them. He turned questioningly to Whiskers, who shrugged. Whiskers admitted that the two men were bitter rivals, although no one quite understood why. But he added that no one knew the plains better than they did. In that case, responded Alvarado, I accept them as my guides.

Alvarado and his soldiers stayed several days in Cicuye, enjoying the hospitality of Whiskers. During that time, the Turk watched and listened to the Spanish captain closely. The guide was curious about the strangers. Over and over, the Turk overheard Alvarado questioning Whiskers impatiently about gold. Was there none in Cicuye? Did Whiskers know where any could be found? The Turk could tell from the eager look on Alvarado's face that gold was very important to the Spanish captain.

From childhood, the Turk had been known for his sharp wits. And his wits now told him he could use the friendship of the newcomers to help himself. The Turk did not like being a captive of Cicuye, but he knew that if he ran away he would be captured and punished severely. Slowly the idea dawned on him that the strangers might offer another way for him to escape. If he could convince them there was gold in Quivera, he might be chosen to lead them on a far longer journey than the one they planned now. He might be chosen to take them all the way across the plains to Quivera itself—his home. He decided to bide his time.

In early October, Alvarado and his guides said

goodbye to Whiskers and traveled eastward for four days until they reached the edge of the huge plains. Alvarado could not imagine how far the plains went, or where they ended. In every direction, as far as the eye could see, stretched short grasses, stirring in the breeze. The land was absolutely flat, and the sky hung over them like a bright blue tent.

The Turk continued to observe Alvarado. He was impressed with Alvarado's courage and daring. The first time Alvarado saw one of the woolly, hump-back cows, he turned his horse away. But he quickly learned how to dodge the animals' cruel horns and to kill them with the Cicuyans' spears. Still, the Turk thought Alvarado sometimes acted too quickly. Once Alvarado was almost thrown when he raced his horse into a group of enraged bulls.

Early one morning, when he was walking beside Alvarado, the Turk pointed into the distance. His home and Sopete's, he reminded Alvarado, lay far away, on the other side of the plains. He asked whether Alvarado had ever heard of Quivera. He commented sadly that he missed his home, which was a large and beautiful city—much grander than Cicuye. In the cities of

Quivera, he said, the people wear gold and silver ornaments and clothes made of rich fabrics.

Alvarado stared at him. The captain's face became red with excitement. There is gold in Quivera? demanded Alvarado. Alvarado had traveled more than a thousand miles in search of the metal and had found nothing. Like others in the army, his nerves were raw from the months of hardship, hunger, and fear. Now, perhaps, their luck was about to change. Perhaps sparkling jewels and gleaming metals lay just beyond the horizon! Tell me more about Quivera! he ordered sharply.

"In my country," answered the Turk, "there is a river in which there are fishes as big as horses and large numbers of very big canoes, with more than twenty rowers on a side, and on the prow they have a great golden eagle."

Quivera sounded as proud and wealthy as the Aztec cities of New Spain! Alvarado could hardly breathe. What about the ruler of the city?

The Turk could see his stories were having the result he wanted. "The lord of my country," he said, weaving a web of clever deceit, "takes his afternoon nap under a great tree on which there hang a great number of little gold bells, which put him to sleep as they swing in the air."

Suddenly Alvarado became suspicious. How do I know any of this is true? he demanded. The Turk had expected this. It is my misfortune, the guide answered, that I have no proof. I was wearing gold bracelets when I was captured by the Cicuyans, and they have never returned these possessions. Please, he begged Alvarado, do not say I told you this, or they will punish me.

But the Turk had misjudged the strength of Alvarado's desire to find gold. Alvarado immediately ordered a return to Cicuye. The moment they arrived, he and his soldiers rushed inside the walls, dragging the Turk and Sopete with them. The captain confronted Whiskers. Where are the bracelets? Alvarado demanded. The Turk says you have stolen his gold bracelets, and I want to see them.

Whiskers, usually calm and dignified, looked angry at this accusation. He rose to his feet. The Turk, he responded, is lying. He pointed at Sopete, whose painted eyes were round with worry. Ask Sopete. Sopete will tell you this is a story. The Turk wants to go home. He thinks if he can convince you there is gold, we will have to set him free.

You are the liar, Alvarado shouted. Sopete

hates the Turk. He will never admit the Turk is telling the truth about something as important as this! Where are the bracelets?

Alvarado and Whiskers stood face to face. They were about the same height and age—both strong, proud, and young. They had almost become friends on the long journey from Cibola to Cicuye. Suddenly, they were bitter enemies. Whiskers put his hand on his spear. He tried once more to explain. If I had gold bracelets, I would give them to you. But there are no gold bracelets in Cicuye. Now leave here.

Seize him, Alvarado ordered his soldiers. Then he turned on the Turk and Sopete. And seize them, too! We can't afford to let any of them escape until we know the truth. The soldiers clapped iron collars and chains on the Turk, Sopete, and Whiskers. Quickly the soldiers hustled their prisoners down the ladders and away from the walls of the town.

The people of Cicuye were stunned. They shot arrows from their walls and shook their fists. They screamed that Alvarado had broken his word and betrayed their friendship. But it was too late. The brash young commander, determined to find gold, rode away with his prisoners.

4

Backwards in Sorrow

Alvarado and his captives traveled as far as Alcanfor, one of the pueblos of Tiguex. There, they were met by López de Cárdenas, who had been sent ahead by Coronado. Captain Cárdenas reported that Coronado was on his way, having decided to spend the winter in the district of Tiguex. Alvarado ordered his prisoners to be kept under constant guard until Coronado arrived.

Coronado reached Alcanfor later in November, exhausted. Severely cold weather made the trip much more difficult than Alvarado's journey in August. Nor was Coronado pleased by the tensions he found brewing in the villages of Tiguex. Because the weather was so icy, Cárdenas had decided to move his troops into the Alcanfor pueblo. To make room for his men, he had ordered all the people of Alcanfor to take only the clothes on their backs and move to a nearby pueblo. Then his soldiers moved inside Alcanfor's warm walls.

Soon after his arrival, Coronado met with Alvarado and the Turk. Coronado wasn't sure Alvarado had been wise to seize the prisoners. Perhaps the young captain had acted rashly, without considering the results. But Coronado generally did not interfere too much in the decisions of his captains. He gave them a task, and left them with the responsibility of carrying it out. Besides, his soldiers had been away from home for more than nine months now. Their patience was stretched to the limit.

Coronado's hopes, too, had soared when he heard the Turk's stories. The Turk had a direct way of speaking that was very convincing. Almost against his will, Coronado found himself sympathizing with Alvarado's harsh methods. True, it would have been better not to create enemies in Cicuye. But this was the first hint of treasure he had heard in months! No wonder Alvarado had acted as he did, thought Coronado.

Watching Coronado's reaction, the Turk decided to slip some new details into his story. He described how the people of Quivera ate their meals. "The common table service of everybody is generally of wrought silver," he explained enthusiastically, "and the pitchers, dishes, and bowls are made of gold." He also claimed an even richer land, called Harahey, lay beyond Quivera. Coronado and Alvarado exchanged glances. This was exciting news, indeed!

To test whether the Turk knew the difference between metals, Coronado showed him some brass. The Turk sensed a trick right away. He smelled the metal, turned it over in his hands, and handed it back to Coronado. That's not gold, he told the General with easy confidence, using the word *achochis* to mean gold. Coronado nodded, feeling jubilant. The Turk's stories just might be true!

That night, Coronado called a meeting of his captains. It is our sworn duty, he reminded them, to do all within our power to find gold for our King and our Viceroy. But we cannot undertake a journey during the winter snows. He scanned their tense, thin faces. Coronado felt so restless to begin he could hardly bear the long months of waiting. He knew they were equally eager. In the spring, he said, we will set out for Quivera with the Turk as our guide. The one named Sopete also has crossed the plains, so he will go along as well. Only when we reach Quivera will we know whether the Turk has told the truth.

He turned to Alvarado. On the way to Quivera, the General said, we will return Whiskers to Cicuye. But in the meanwhile, Whiskers must remain here as our prisoner, along with the Turk and Sopete. Perhaps prison will force a confession from the one who is lying! Then Coronado asked Alvarado to speak with Whiskers one more time about the matter of the bracelets.

Once again Alvarado questioned Whiskers, and once again Whiskers said he knew nothing about any bracelets. Whiskers was returned to the gloomy room that was his jail. His arms and legs were chained. He slept on a hard, narrow bench built into the mud and stone wall. His only contact with the outside world was a soldier named Cervantes, who brought him food and water. Cervantes was a jittery man who kept looking over his shoulder for danger. He believed the prisoners from Cicuye possessed evil powers. He hopped in and out of Whiskers' prison as quickly as a scared rabbit.

Whiskers had no idea how long he remained there. Days and nights flowed together. A month passed by like a dream. Then one morning in late December, as Whiskers dozed, three soldiers burst into the room. We'll show you what happens to people who defy us, growled one of them. The soldier pushed Whiskers ahead of him into the blinding sunshine. Whiskers saw Cervantes hustling the Turk and Sopete in the same direction. The prisoners were forced onto horses and made to ride swiftly across the icy fields toward Arenal, one of the neighboring pueblos. As they approached, Whiskers could see clouds of black smoke rising over the walls.

They dismounted and hastened toward the pueblo. The soldier's hand was tight on Whiskers' elbow. A hideous smell made Whiskers gag and choke. They stopped just outside the pueblo's walls, and for a moment Whiskers couldn't see through the smoky haze. Then his eyes focused, and he staggered backward in sorrow and shock. In front of him, in a huge pile, lay the bones and blackened flesh of many bodies. The warriors of Arenal had been tied to stakes and burned alive. Whiskers' teeth chattered from the horror of the scene as well as from the brutal cold. Slowly he lifted his eyes until they met the Turk's. The Turk's eyes blazed with anger. Sopete had covered his face with his hands.

The people of this pueblo, snarled the soldier, murdered one of our men. They killed dozens of our horses—horses that belonged to the King of Spain! How are we supposed to survive in this wilderness without our horses? He shook his fist at Whiskers, as though the Cicuyan had been responsible.

As calmly as possible, Whiskers asked in sign language whether Coronado had ordered the brutal punishment. The soldier was glad to supply the details. The General put Captain Cárdenas in charge, he answered. The captain asked the people of Arenal for peace, but they refused—twice. Instead, they took up arms against us. He laughed out loud, creating an ugly sound. When the warriors of Arenal made war against us, he continued, the General ordered Captain Cárdenas to take no prisoners. You can see how Captain Cárdenas deals with such matters!

He paused and looked in Whiskers' eyes. The General himself wanted you to see this sight, he hissed. He wanted you to understand what can happen to those who defy us! With an abrupt turn, the soldier ordered the prisoners back to their horses, and they returned to Alcanfor.

The rest of the long winter, confined at Alcanfor, Whiskers couldn't get the massacre at Arenal out of his mind. The blackened bodies haunted him. Then, just when Whiskers had given up hope of freedom, Alvarado at last arrived to release him. One by one, the captain removed the chains from Whiskers' arms and legs. You're going home to Cicuye, Alvarado said. We will stop at Cicuye along the way to Quivera. There is no longer any reason to hold you hostage. We will soon know the truth for ourselves.

Whiskers stumbled into the daylight. A fresh breeze greeted him. He inhaled deeply, hungry for the sweet spring air. He had thought he might not live through the winter, and now he was going home. In front of him, he saw Coronado in his golden helmet and armor, riding a glossy horse.

Four months had passed since the massacre at Arenal. It was now April 1541, and Coronado felt relieved to be departing for Quivera. The massacre at Arenal had set off a war that had raged in Tiguex through the whole winter. Finally, the inhabitants of the district had been crushed.

We live among strangers in a foreign land,

thought Coronado. During the winter, deep snows and fierce storms keep us prisoners, with few supplies to last until spring. During the summer, our skins blister with heat, and our throats ache from thirst. We are never safe. If we do not act with strength and speed, we will soon fall victim to starvation or attack.

Slowly, Coronado turned his head and surveyed the army. A number of his soldiers were wounded. Their armor was rusted; their clothing in rags. Yet assembled like this, on a sunny spring morning, they remained an impressive force. More than a thousand people—soldiers, servants, and Indian allies from New Spain—milled before him. Out of the corner of his eye, he saw the Turk, Sopete, and Whiskers—all released from their chains. The air was filled with the restless whinny of a thousand horses and the mournful bleat of five thousand sheep.

In a long line, like a shiny, slithering snake, the army began to move. They were on their way to Cicuye. It was April 23, 1541.

5

Whiskers' Wrath

The people of Cicuye rejoiced to see Whiskers, for they had been certain he was dead. The army camped outside the pueblo's walls while Coronado's soldiers collected supplies and clothing for the long journey. Whiskers was very warm and kind to them. No one could have guessed the young chief was planning revenge.

One night, shortly after the army reached Cicuye, a sudden noise startled the Turk from a sound sleep. Before he could scream, a hand was clapped over his mouth. A tall Cicuyan led him to a room deep inside the pueblo's walls and left him there. It was a moment the Turk had long feared. He stood face to face with Whiskers.

There were no soldiers nearby to protect him from Whiskers' wrath.

But Whiskers didn't move. He didn't draw his spear or strike the Turk. Instead, he spoke in a voice of icy calm. You have convinced these strangers, stated Whiskers, there is gold in Quivera. What do you think will happen when they discover you have lied? Do you think they will set you free in your homeland?

Whiskers began to stalk around the room. Now you are an honored guide who rides at the head of the army. But do you remember how they kept you in chains all winter? Do you remember how they killed the warriors at Arenal? We must rid ourselves of these strangers before they destroy us.

The Turk felt a powerful mix of feelings—fear, confusion, and excitement. Like Whiskers, he could not forget the scene at Arenal. His hatred of the strangers had grown stronger every day.

Whiskers saw a spark of interest in the Turk's eyes. What I ask, said Whiskers, will mean almost certain death for you. But it will make you a hero among the peoples of Cibola, Tiguex, Cicuye, and Quivera. He moved so close to the Turk that their noses almost touched. Take the strangers onto the plains and lose them, Whiskers commanded, so their horses will die when their provisions run out, and they will be so weak that if they ever return they will be killed without any trouble. Thus we can take revenge for what has been done to us.

The Turk's mind raced ahead. He knew there was a good chance he could do it. The sameness of the plains confused even experienced travelers like himself. He began to speak as he formed his thoughts. Quivera, the Turk said, lies northeast. I will lead the army directly east. Before long, they will wander in circles, going nowhere. They will die of hunger and thirst.

And Sopete? demanded Whiskers. Will he also help with this plan?

No, said the Turk firmly. If we confide in him, he will tell the strangers, out of his hatred for me. But what difference can it make if he complains about a wrong direction! He is my enemy. They expect him to disagree with me.

Then it is settled, said Whiskers. I will give the strangers a third guide who will stand by your story. Young Xabe will agree there is much gold in Quivera—although perhaps not quite so much as *you* say. And with that promise, Whiskers sent the Turk back into the dark night.

The army departed for Quivera a few days later. Xabe, a slim, teenage boy, went along with them, chattering about the gold they would find. The Turk led everyone, traveling even ahead of Coronado and Alvarado. Sopete followed at the very back of the column, grumbling about the Turk to anyone who would listen.

Four days out of Cicuye, the army came to a deep river. It took another four days to build a bridge strong enough to hold a thousand humans and many thousands of animals. On the other side of the river stretched the limitless plains.

Although Alvarado had warned Coronado about what to expect, the General found it hard to believe his own eyes. Wherever they went, the short, stubby grass sprang up again, like the waves of the sea. It left no trace that the vast army had ever passed. The horizon circled them like a bowl, exactly the same in all directions. During the day, they saw white-spotted deer and rabbits. Sometimes the army was surrounded by hundreds of huge, bearded, hump-back cows. As a result, hunters could find plenty of animals to kill for food. But there was a terrible shortage of water, and of corn to feed the horses.

At night, all around them, they heard the eerie

howl of white wolves. If someone failed to return to camp, soldiers blew trumpets, beat drums, and fired guns. Without these sounds, a man might never find his way back. After circling and circling, he might drop from exhaustion. Then he would become food for the vultures that soared overhead.

About ten days after crossing the river, the Turk spied pointed shapes in the distance. As he drew closer, the pointed shapes turned into tents. From his earlier travels, the Turk knew he was approaching some Querechos, a people who lived on the plains. The Turk thought the Querechos were an odd people, for they did not live in settled villages. Instead, they traveled wherever the hump-back cows went, carrying their tents with them. They ate the cows and made their tents and clothes from the animals' skins. But the Turk also remembered that the Querechos were a good people and very loyal friends.

The Turk knew their language and decided to trust them now. He quickly approached their camp and told them his story. He briefly described the events at Cibola, Cicuye, and Tiguex and asked for the Querechos' help.

When Coronado and some soldiers rode up a

short while later, the Querechos were very polite. Using sign language, they generously invited the General to share some soup made from the hump-back cows. They listened to his questions, and they answered just as the Turk had told them. When Coronado asked whether there were any large settlements, a man who looked wise and well-traveled responded. "There is a very large river which lies over where the sun comes from." He pointed directly east. "One can go along this river through an inhabited region for ninety days without a break from settlement to settlement."

Coronado nodded in satisfaction. Such large settlements, he thought, must be wealthy. And the Querechos had pointed east, the very direction the Turk and Xabe had been taking the army all along.

When the rest of Coronado's captains arrived, however, they were not as satisfied. Several of them had formed strong doubts about the Turk. One declared that Cervantes had seen the Turk talking with the Devil. Nonsense! said Coronado. Another captain described how Sopete called the Turk a rascal. There is no love between them, Coronado admitted. A third warned Coronado not to trust the word of the Querechos, since the Turk had met with them first. Coronado listened to all of their doubts, feeling angry and upset. Did they think he wanted to remain on these plains forever? Did they think he had no doubts himself? How he longed to be back in his beautiful home in New Spain, enjoying the company of his family. But he forced himself to speak with calm authority.

What choice do we have? he asked. We have promised our Viceroy and our King to find gold. It is our duty to explore every possibility. Should we give up like cowards and go home? Only in time will we know the truth. We must be patient and continue with courage.

Yet as more days passed, worry began to hound Coronado morning and night. They had left Tiguex on April 23, and had stopped only briefly in Cicuye. It was already late May. If the words of the Querechos had been true, wouldn't they have seen signs of settlement by now? Instead, the General watched the members of his army grow weak and ill before his very eyes. One man wandered away into the empty horizon, never to return. Cárdenas broke his arm and, crazed from pain, had to be removed from command. Diego López was appointed army-master in his place. A wild storm arose, with hailstones as huge as boulders. It battered helmets, tore tents, and wounded animals. Meanwhile, the army's horses shrank to skeletons from the lack of food.

Early one morning, in the gray dawn, Sopete approached Coronado. May I speak with you, Sopete asked, in sign language. Coronado was surprised, since he had rarely talked directly with Sopete. Please believe me, said the guide, when I say the Turk is a liar. He is leading you in the wrong direction. The boy, Xabe, only repeats whatever the Turk tells him.

Coronado didn't trust the Turk, but neither did he trust Sopete. He knew the hatred between the two guides was as bitter as poison. But before Coronado could think of what to say, Sopete threw himself on the ground. He pounded the earth with his fists. His voice became a howl. Cut off my head, now! Sopete shouted. What does it matter? We will all die together here on the plains. Quivera does not lie in the direction of the rising sun! He rolled in the grass as though in extreme pain. The Turk is leading you astray, he hissed. Cut off my head! Cut off my head! I swear I am telling you the truth.

Coronado bent down and pulled Sopete to a standing position. Be quiet, said Coronado sharply. I'm not going to kill you for your words. You've done nothing to deserve death. He paused. The time is coming soon when I will have to make a decision about the Turk. He looked across the plains. Some soldiers were mounting their horses. Others were beginning to trudge wearily east, toward the great orange ball on the horizon. To Coronado, the rising sun looked frightening as it burst into the sky. Did Quivera lie in that direction or in a different direction altogether?

This is a dangerous country, Coronado murmured, almost to himself. There are no more landmarks on these plains than if we had been swallowed up in the sea—not a stone, nor a bit of rising ground, nor a tree, nor a shrub, nor anything to go by. We could die here, he thought, and never see our homes or families in New Spain again. Each passing day, each long week, takes a toll on our strength and spirit.

He strode away from Sopete. Before long, the General stated firmly, I will make my decision.

6

City of Straw

The chance to make a decision came sooner than Coronado had expected. As he sometimes had in the past, he sent a small party of soldiers ahead to explore. They returned with news—they had spotted a group of people not too far away. These people, reported the soldiers, seemed to live like the Querechos, traveling with their tents behind the hump-back cows. When asked, all three guides—who rarely agreed about any-thing—agreed that the wanderers were probably Teyas. And then the Turk offered to speak with the Teyas himself, since he knew a little of their language. But even before Sopete could object,

49

Coronado shook his head. He had decided to pay a visit to the Teyas without the Turk present.

As he rode up, the Teyas came out of their tents to greet him. Using sign language, Coronado asked about the direction of large settlements. They seemed puzzled. But after some confusion, they understood his meaning. They waved their hands in disagreement. They made it clear that no settlements lay in the direction of the rising sun. There were no trails there either. Only the vast plains. Then the Teyas pointed north. In that direction, they assured Coronado, lay settlements. Although they hadn't spoken with Sopete, their information confirmed his story, not the Turk's.

By now, late May, Coronado and his men had been traveling almost a month on the plains. The Teyas directed the General toward a deep canyon where the army could rest and find protection from the heat and fierce storms. On May 26, Coronado called a meeting of his captains. Diego López—who was now second-in-command—Cárdenas, Alvarado, and the others huddled together, listening closely. Our supplies are running out, the General told them. There is no way of obtaining anything we need. I have decided to go in search of Quivera myself, with thirty horse-men. The rest of the army must return to Tiguex.

Word of the decision spread like wildfire. As soon as they learned about the plan, a group of soldiers came to Coronado's torn and shabby tent. They gathered around, begging the General to change his mind.

We will never let you go without us, shouted one soldier. Never, echoed the crowd. We would rather die with you than leave you, added another soldier. Coronado surveyed them with affection. Many of them, he knew, were very loyal. Others hated to retreat without seeing the end of the adventure. Still others wanted to be the first to reach Quivera in case there was any gold. You are very brave, he said. But I have no choice. We have few supplies, and I must protect your lives.

Who will you choose? demanded a man who stood at the front of the crowd. Coronado had given this much thought. The answer seemed clear. "I will choose those who seem the most dependable and who have the best horses," he replied. Then he spoke very clearly. When we go, we will change direction. We will travel north instead of east.

The Turk, who had been standing at the back of the crowd, felt his heart miss a beat. At Coronado's words, the guide realized his plans had come to nothing. When they turned north, the strangers would find Quivera. Still, the Turk resolved not to give up hope. He would find another way to destroy the strangers.

The next day, the army—including the wounded and weary Cárdenas—started back to Tiguex. The young boy, Xabe, returned with them, on Coronado's orders. A small band of men, led by Coronado himself, set out across the plains to the north. Diego López traveled just in back of Coronado. Alvarado proudly rode his magnificent horse a little way behind. Sopete also had a place at the front, but the Turk trailed at the rear. Once again, he wore heavy chains.

The Thirty traveled for a little more than a month, growing weaker and weaker from their diet of meat and muddy water. Coronado tried to keep up the spirit of his soldiers as best he could, but it was difficult. As they traveled, they saw no signs of wealthy settlements. They saw only hump-back cows.

At the end of June, they reached a river that flowed northeast. They followed it for several days until, in the distance, they could see signs of a village or town. They had at last arrived at their goal—Quivera. As they entered the first settlement, in early July, Coronado closed his eyes in disappointment. Instead of large and beautiful stone houses, like the ones the Turk had described, they found one-story straw cabins. The people of Quivera—men, women, and children—poured from their homes to see the strangers. They were full of curiosity. They had heard about these men from the Querechos, the Teyas, and other wanderers of the plains. One of their leaders approached Coronado to welcome him. The Quiveran wore a large copper ornament around his neck. Coronado feared that gleaming bit of metal was as close to gold as anything he would see.

For twenty-five days the Thirty explored the entire extent of Quivera. Like the people of the pueblos, the Quiverans lived in settled villages. But their homes were round, each with a single story and a roof of straw. The countryside was beautiful and lush. In some ways, it reminded Coronado of Spain. Fruits and vegetables were plentiful. There were plums—as delicious as those of Castile—grapes, nuts, mulberries, oats, and wild marjoram.

But there was no gold to be found anywhere. As the days passed, Coronado's captains became

angrier and angrier. Kill the Turk, demanded Diego López and several others. Coronado could see no point in it. "What honor would be gained by killing the Indian?" he questioned.

Coronado changed his mind at the last Quiveran village they visited, where he requested corn for their hungry horses. The Quiverans refused to give him any. Sopete stepped forward to find out why. I am your countryman, Sopete said to the Quiverans. I have brought the strangers here under my protection. Why do you act in such a way?

The Quiverans hesitated and exchanged fearful glances. But as Sopete continued to press, an old man finally answered. Because of the Turk, said the Quiveran. The Turk said the strangers could never survive on the plains without their animals. He said we should give their beasts no food. The Quiveran paused and then continued. He urged us to kill them!

Coronado immediately summoned the Turk. As he walked toward Coronado, dragging his heavy chains, the Turk made up his mind. There was no longer any point in lying. Coronado had reached the last Quiveran settlement. He had seen there was no gold. He had found out about the Turk's plans to destroy the Thirty.

Coronado looked into the Turk's eyes. You were my chosen guide, he said. I trusted you. I have refused to have you killed, even though my captains advised it. Why have you done this? Why did you lead the army onto the plains with these tales of Quivera? Why did you lead us east, away from Quivera, instead of north? Why, even now, do you plan our deaths?

The Turk stood straight and proud. He began to speak. He reminded Coronado how Alvarado had seized Whiskers, chief of the Cicuye, and made him a prisoner. He also reminded Coronado how Cárdenas had massacred the people of Arenal. Then he repeated what Whiskers had said to him. "The people at Cicuye," he said, "asked me to lead you onto the plains and lose you, so the horses would die when your provisions ran out, and you would be so weak whenever you returned that you would be killed without any trouble. Thus they could take revenge for what had been done to them. This is the reason I led you astray."

Coronado heard his captains gasp aloud in response to the Turk's confession. Coronado himself trembled with anger, but the rage quickly passed. The Turk, after all, had been protecting his people, just as Coronado always acted to protect the interests of the Viceroy, the King, and his soldiers. Yet there was one question the Turk hadn't answered completely. Hardly daring still to hope, Coronado asked it. And the gold? he said. Is there any gold in this vast country of yours?

The Turk spoke simply. "I do not know where there is any of it," he answered.

Now Coronado knew he could no longer save the Turk from death. If he tried, he would risk losing his soldiers' loyalty. Moreover, the Turk's persistence in his plan presented too great a threat. In the next village or the next town, the Quiveran would continue to plot their destruction. Without hesitation, Coronado ordered the Turk to be executed. That night, Alvarado and López took the prisoner from his tent and put him to death.

By the next day, Coronado's thoughts had already moved on to the next stage of their journey. Soon, he knew, the sizzling summer heat would turn to autumn. It would be dangerous for the little group of thirty to be trapped in Quivera by the cold weather. The Quiverans might take it into their heads to carry out the Turk's plans. The Thirty must return to Tiguex to rejoin the rest of the army.

Before leaving Quivera, Coronado went with his men to a beautiful place he had admired. It was a green meadow beside a rushing stream, with blue flax flowering everywhere. He wore his full armor, and the sun glinted off his golden helmet. As he watched, several soldiers erected a great wooden cross. On it were carved the words: "Francisco Vázquez de Coronado, general of an expedition, reached this place." Coronado felt proud to see the huge cross raised against the cloudless, sparkling sky. We found no gold here, he said to his men. But anyone who journeys through Quivera will now see we too have explored this country.

When Coronado departed for Tiguex in mid-August, he allowed Sopete to remain home in Quivera, as promised. Sopete was very pleased with the way things turned out. He had always known the Turk was a rascal. Now the strangers knew it, too.

7

Dark Moments

Coronado shook his head, worried, and then continued writing. It was difficult to think of what to say. He was composing a letter to the King, informing him of all the events that had passed. How could Coronado admit that he, a great general, had been fooled by the lies of the Turk, Xabe, and the Querechos? He had no choice but to describe honestly the difficulties and mistakes of the expedition to Quivera. With determination, he focused on the task:

"I remained twenty-five days in this province of Quivera, so as to see and explore the country and also to find out whether there was anything beyond which could be of service to Your

Majesty, because the guides who had brought me had given me an account of other provinces beyond this.

"And what I am sure of is that there is not any gold nor any other metal in all that country. And the other things of which they had told me are nothing but little villages, and in many of these they do not plant anything and do not have any houses except of skins and sticks, and they wander around with the cows.

"So the account they gave me was false, because they wanted to persuade me to go there with the whole force, believing that as the way was through such uninhabited deserts, and from the lack of water, they would get us where we and our horses would die of hunger. And the guides confessed this, and said they had done it by the advice and orders of the natives of these provinces.

"And thus, after having heard the account of what was beyond, which I have given above, I returned to these provinces to provide for the force I had sent back here and to give Your Majesty an account of what this country amounts to, because I wrote Your Majesty that I would do so when I went there."

Coronado reread the letter and dated it—October 20, 1541. He planned to give it to Cárdenas to take to Viceroy Mendoza. Mendoza would see that it was sent across the sea to Spain. Cárdenas was still too ill and weak to return to his duties as army-master. He had also received word of a family member's death in New Spain. So Coronado had given him permission to make the journey home. This time, Cárdenas would be the messenger who visited Mendoza and Doña Beatriz.

Cárdenas departed for New Spain a few weeks later, in November, carrying Coronado's letter. Ten other men, too badly wounded to survive another winter in Tiguex or another journey to Quivera, went with him. They were a mournful little company of soldiers, with blood-stained bandages and missing limbs. Sadly, Coronado bade farewell to Cárdenas, wondering if he would ever see the captain again. Coronado sensed the coming winter would be a cruel one.

The icy chill of winter was already in the air. The full army, including Coronado's Thirty, had set up headquarters once again in Tiguex. There was great unhappiness among them. Young Xabe had met the Thirty on their return from Quivera in mid-September. The boy had looked innocently surprised at their tale of the Turk's betrayal. No gold at Quivera? Xabe had demanded. Had they looked everywhere? Had they gone on to Harahey, the land beyond Quivera?

Listening to Xabe, some of the soldiers who had returned with the main army grew frustrated. They decided the Thirty had missed something. You should have gone a little way farther, they grumbled. Surely there was gold, if only you had gone just a little farther. A group had come to Coronado to convince him to try again. You know the plains so well, they said. It would be easy for you to lead us across them in the spring. Coronado agreed to do so, even though he had little hope. He felt he owed it to his brave soldiers, the Viceroy, and the King.

As Coronado had feared, the winter was long and hard. Food grew scarce, and the army's clothes were in shreds. Some soldiers were practically naked in the bitter cold. Coronado felt cooped up, like a bird in a cage. The only real activity he enjoyed was exercising his horses, which he did daily.

One freezing December morning he felt particularly restless. When he walked outside, the air gave him energy. He breathed deeply and happily stroked the silky neck of his favorite horse. That day, he had challenged one of his captains, Don Rodrigo Maldonado, to a race. The two men mounted and were off in an instant, their horses swift as the wind. Coronado pulled ahead and looked back triumphantly. Suddenly, the world turned upside down—he had been thrown. With thundering hoofs, Maldonado's horse was upon Coronado and struck him. Everything went black.

Days later Coronado still lay in bed, ill and near death. He moved in and out of consciousness. He overheard people talking. They said he had been thrown because his saddle strap had worn through. Will I die here all alone, he wondered, far from my family? He longed for his wife. He could feel her hands on his feverish forehead. Sometimes, in the night, he would see her moving about the room, bringing him fresh water, bending down to kiss him. Then he would realize that it had only been a dream. She was more than a thousand miles away in New Spain.

During these dark moments, he thought often of the words a fortuneteller had once said to him in Spain. He had still been quite a young man at the time. How promising his life had looked then!

But the fortuneteller had warned, "Coronado, you will become a powerful lord in distant lands. But you will one day suffer from a great fall from which you will never recover."

During his illness, Coronado heard other news that disturbed him deeply. For nearly two years, his soldiers had been united in their goals and loyalty. Now they quarreled like animals. Some wanted only to return to New Spain as soon as Coronado was well enough to lead the way. Others refused to think about leaving. What, go away now? they demanded. Absolutely not! We must go back to Quivera in the spring and continue to look for gold.

Lying there, feverish and sick, Coronado felt torn between two desires. For the sake of Viceroy Mendoza, the King, and the future, he wanted to go on. But oh, how he longed to return home!

At last he was well enough to get out of his bed. For several days in a row he sat up and walked around for a few hours each morning. One morning, as he was sitting and reading, a noise startled him. When he turned around, he saw López de Cárdenas standing beside him. Coronado caught his breath. What was Cárdenas doing here? Cárdenas had returned home, with letters, to New Spain! He had left in November, several months before. Surely this was a dream, just as when Doña Beatriz appeared. But Cárdenas reached out his hand, and Coronado took it. It was flesh and blood.

I have returned to bring you bad news, General, said Cárdenas. I have waited some weeks to tell you, in order to allow you to build up your strength. Cárdenas shuddered with the horror of what he had seen. It is news from the south. It is news from the Suya Valley.

Coronado could guess from his captain's face what had happened. More than a year and a half ago, Coronado's army had passed through the Suya Valley on the way to Cibola. Coronado had left a group of soldiers there to start a town and guard the way back to New Spain.

Our people made many enemies in the Suya Valley, moaned Cárdenas. All the people of the area have risen in rebellion. They murdered three soldiers and more than twenty horses. The town has been abandoned.

When I learned what had happened, Cárdenas continued, I came back to tell you. If you and the army do not move homeward as soon as the weather allows, the route back will be cut off entirely. You cannot spend another spring and summer in these lands. The revolt may spread and bring destruction on all of us.

Coronado heard him only faintly, as though the captain were very far away. Then blackness once again fell upon the General. With the shock of the terrible news, his illness had returned.

When Coronado was at last well enough, and spring had thawed the ice on the river, the army prepared to depart for home. At daybreak on April 1, 1542, the General rose and put on his armor. It was the only gold he had to take back to New Spain, the only gold he had for Mendoza. He walked outside, mounted his horse, and looked out over Tiguex. In the rosy morning sun and hazy air, the villages spread before him loomed as grandly as palaces. Perhaps this is how the stories about cities of gold first started—a trick of the sun.

Behind Coronado gathered the captains, soldiers, and allies of the army. They were threadbare and exhausted. Yet, in the two years of the expedition, Coronado had lost fewer than fifty of the thousand people who had marched with him from New Spain. He knew he could be proud of that record.

He let his mind play back across the two years. He had found no gold. The war at Tiguex had destroyed many Cicuyan lives. Coronado had hoped to be a less harsh conqueror than Pizarro and Cortés had been. But he knew many of his acts, and those of his captains, had caused hatred that would last a long, long time. Coronado saw the flashing eyes of the Turk, just before his death. The Turk had risked his life to protect his people.

Yet Coronado knew that his army had also shown great courage. They had traveled across lands no European had ever seen. They had faced war, starvation, fierce storms, and something even more terrifying—the unknown.

When they started out from New Spain, no one had any idea what they might find in the deserts and wilderness of the north. Now they knew, for they had seen it with their own eyes. He thought of the walls of Cibola, the thundering hump-back cows, and the Querechos, who made their tents with the cows' skins. He saw the miles of grassy plains the army had crossed between Tiguex and Quivera.

He, Coronado, had a precious gift to give Mendoza—not gold, but knowledge of the vast

and varied lands that stretched north of New Spain. Alas, he feared it was a gift that Mendoza would not value.

Coronado raised his arms high over his head. At his signal, the drums and trumpets sounded. With banners waving, the army set out once more, this time for home.

Epilogue

As the fortuneteller had predicted, Coronado never fully recovered from his fall. When he reached New Spain in the autumn of 1542, he was greeted by a very disappointed Mendoza. Later Coronado was accused of misconduct for the manner in which he commanded the expedition. He was charged with misdeeds ranging from the massacre at Arenal to abandoning the lands he had discovered. Although he was asked to pay a fine for some small offenses, in February 1546, he was found not guilty of misconduct. He was allowed to keep a minor government office. Eight years later, Coronado died at the early age of 44.

Coronado's reports of his travels described North America's rich variety of people, lands, and animals. The names of Cicuye, Quivera, and Cibola began to appear on maps. About fifty years after Coronado's expedition, Spanish explorers, traders, officials, and adventurers set out from New Spain to form Spanish settlements in the north.

Although there are disagreements about many of the details of Coronado's journey, there is agreement on some things. The people of Cibola were the ancestors of the Zuñi Indians. A group of soldiers led by López de Cárdenas were the first Europeans to see the Grand Canyon. On the site of Cicuye, home of Whiskers, can still be seen the ruins of the pueblo of Pecos. Readers may already have guessed that the hump-back cows were buffalo. And by the time Coronado had reached Quivera, he had traveled almost to the center of what later became the continental United States. He had arrived at a place we call Kansas.

There were several accounts of the journey written by Coronado's soldiers, but the most detailed is by Pedro Castañeda. Castañeda wrote twenty years after the expedition. He said he wanted people to know exactly what had happened during the journey. And although he was disappointed that the journey had not made him rich, Castañeda could still boast to his readers in Europe and New Spain ". . . we were the first who discovered it and brought word of it."

Afterword

When we hear about the actions of people from the past, we're sometimes surprised and puzzled about why they acted the way they did. Much as we might want to, we can't hop aboard a time machine to find out exactly why a person made a certain choice or behaved a certain way. We have to depend a lot on the clues they left behind and a little on guesswork.

I've made some judgments and guesses about what the people portrayed in this book felt and thought. I've based my ideas on documents from the time as well as the work of more recent historians. Even the Spanish, who wrote a fair amount, didn't always leave an exact record of their conversations. In the preceding chapters, when you read a passage that was in quotation marks, it was an exact, or almost exact, quote taken from a letter or report. If a conversation wasn't in quotation marks, it was based on many clues and a little guesswork about what may have happened or been said.

In general, this story relies on three main sources: *The Journey of Coronado*, a collection of original writings by people from Coronado's time, edited by George Parker Winship, *Coronado, Knight of Pueblos and Plains*; a biography of Coronado by Herbert E. Bolton; and *Coronado's Quest*, a biography of Coronado written by A. Grove Day. Each of these books was helpful in putting together the story I've told here.

Notes

Page 2 The description of Coronado's character is based on accounts from his time and from those in later biographies. Until the end of the expedition, his army seems to have been remarkably devoted to him. He was a strong leader, a loving husband, and a courageous servant of the Viceroy and King. He was neither as blindly greedy nor as cruel as many others who set out to explore, conquer, and settle the Americas.

Pages 17–18 We do not know exactly how Coronado made the decision to send Alvarado to Cicuye or where the General made the decision. But he was a superb horseman, and he spent a lot of time riding. It would have been very much in character for him to have taken such a ride to clear his head to make an important decision.

Page 23 We have no record of the first meeting of Alvarado, the Turk, and Sopete. However, the intense dislike between the Turk and Sopete was immediately obvious, and it was well known to soldiers serving in Coronado's army at the time.

One source suggests that the Turk may have been Pawnee, and that Sopete may have been Wichita, implying that this might be the reason for their dislike of each other. But no one knows why they didn't like each other, only that they didn't.

Page 24 According to Herbert Bolton, the Turk probably first made up the stories of gold in order to escape from Cicuye and return to his home. What the Turk says about Quivera is taken from Castañeda's history of the expedition. Castañeda did not record the exact words of the Turk's conversation with Alvarado. However, the Turk often repeated the same stories over and over, so I've taken the liberty of using the words of a later description by the Turk here.

Page 28 Reports on the imprisonment of Whiskers, the Turk, and Sopete vary from source to source. One source suggests that Alvarado and the Turk first met with Coronado in Tiguex, and that Alvarado afterwards returned to Cicuye for Whiskers. Another source states that Alvarado seized the prisoners on his own authority, before meeting with Coronado. This story followed the second source because the reckless nature of the imprisonment seemed more in keeping with Alvarado's than Coronado's character.

There was also another person taken prisoner—an old man known as "the governor." Given the number of characters already involved, I chose not to introduce him here.

Pages 34–35 There were many reasons why the people of Tiguex rose against the army. The Tiguas were angry about the demands of the Spanish army for food, clothing, and shelter. They were also angry that prisoners had been taken at Cicuye. In addition, Bolton reports that some Spanish soldiers treated the Tiguas cruelly both before and after the uprising. In particular, dogs were set on Whiskers to make him confess about the gold bracelets. During the 1500s, violence and terror were acceptable ways to discipline, punish, and investigate.

Pages 39–41 There is no description of this meeting between Whiskers and the Turk. But, according to Castañeda, the Turk was convinced by the Cicuyans to behave as he did. The words Whiskers here speaks to the Turk are the very ones the Turk later speaks to Coronado, documented by Castañeda. Whiskers' instructions were probably given in pretty much the same terms.

Although we can't know Whiskers' reasons with any certainty, the Cicuyan indeed assigned Xabe to Coronado, and the young Quiveran supported the idea of gold in Quivera until the army finally departed for New Spain.

Pages 43–45 Some historians suggest that the Querechos may have been Apache Indians.

Page 48 Coronado's thoughts here about the plains are taken almost directly from the later letter he sent to Mendoza about the expedition to Quivera.

Page 49 According to George Winship, the Teyas may have been Comanches.

Pages 51–52 Although Coronado specifically chose thirty horsemen, he also traveled with six foot soldiers and several servants. Bolton calls them the "Chosen Thirty," and I've taken the liberty of calling them simply the Thirty.

Page 58 We have no record of the actual spot where Coronado erected his wooden cross in what is now Kansas, nor has it ever been found.

Page 67 López de Cárdenas indeed returned with bad news, but we do not know whether he was the one who actually told Coronado. However, since Cárdenas had witnessed events firsthand, it seemed logical that he would be.

Barbara Weisberg is a poet, biographer, and freelance editor who lives in New York City. She is the author of *Susan B. Anthony,* a biography for young adults.